250 SPEED DATING QUESTIONS

YOUR COMPANION GUIDE TO DATING SUCCESS

Published by Glowworm Press

7 Nuffield Way

Abingdon OX14 1RL

By Connor Champion

Speed Dating Questions

Armed with the list of questions within this book, your speed dating night is bound to be successful. Use this book and you will never be tongue tied, and you will be on your way to finding out really useful information about the people you meet, which will help to let you decide whether you want to see that person again. Using this book will ensure you not only have a fun and successful speed dating evening, but will also help you on the right path towards a meaningful long term relationship.

With this truly fantastic list of really good Speed Dating questions, you will be able to discover more about your dates, their hobbies and interests, their personality and what makes them tick. You will also find out the best time to ask these questions so that the other person does not feel like they are being interviewed. This book will enable you to establish whether you have any common interests and most importantly if there is chemistry between you and to see if there is a spark.

Table of Contents

What others are saying about this successful book

"when i had my first initial speed dating experience a while ago I thought I had a plan of what to say and how to put myself across. I have to admit that I crashed and burned and came out with no matches and walked out with not very much confidence! this book really helps get you in the correct mindset and I would highly recommend reading this to anyone, as it helps get you in the right mind set before you even arrive at the event! my next speed dating experience was much more successful after reading this! :)."

Rebecca Probert, UK

"speed dating can be intimidating but a lot of fun as well. with limited time, the way you present and the questions that you ask are vital. rather than asking some random boring questions i wanted to get prepared and focus on interesting and revealing conversation starters. with this book i feel ready for the next dating adventure!"

J.Blythe, USA

"This is a good guideline for anyone- male or female -to read, over and over. Many great questions if you're out there dating to weed out what you want and don't want. Also gives many "icebreaker" questions, in case the situation is uncomfortable. I highly recommend it!"

D.Takao- Sacramento, USA

Chapter 1: Introduction

We can all get a little stuck for words and tongue tied from time to time. If you ever get stuck for something to say at a speed dating event, simply use some of these questions to kick start your conversation, and before you know it the conversation will start to flow again and it will soon be just like talking to an old friend you have known for years.

In this book you will find a cracking list of really good Speed Dating questions, and you will also find out the best time to ask these questions so that the other person does not feel like they are being interviewed.

Many hours and many nights have been spent asking speed daters what makes a good question and what doesn't and establishing what are the best questions to ask at a Speed Dating evening.

Here we list a staggering 250 questions – possibly the largest collection of speed dating questions anywhere - all of which will help you find out more about the person you are talking to, and also help you not only enjoy the evening more, but also establish whether you want to see that person again.

Chapter 2: What is Speed Dating?

Speed Dating is ideal for you if you lead a busy life, don't have much spare time and want to meet new people in a fun, safe environment. Most people who go speed dating are professionals who want to improve their chances of meeting the right person. They're generally normal, attractive people with varied interests who normally mix with the same group of friends and work colleagues and rarely get the opportunity to meet many new people in one go.

Speed Dating is all about enjoying an evening meeting like-minded singles who live near you and who want to find someone new.

Speed Dating is an opportunity to meet and date a number of other singles your age, who are serious about wanting to be in a relationship. You will date each person for typically three or four minutes, giving you the opportunity to decide if you want to see that person again.

Four minutes per date turns out to be the perfect amount of time. Four minutes is short enough to leave your date wanting more if they are interested and four minutes is also not too long if the other person turns out to be uninteresting to you.

Four minutes is the right amount of time to decide whether you're prepared to invest more time in follow up emails and phone calls to land a real date. Four minutes per date also enables you to meet many people in one night without getting completely worn out!

With speed dating, everyone on the night will be single and everyone is there to meet other people. At a speed dating evening you will have just enough time with each person to decide whether or not you would like to see them again, and you will only be put in contact with the people you want to meet who also want to meet you again.

At the Speed Dating event

Upon arrival at a Speed Dating event, you will be checked in and given a personalised badge with a number on it. You will be given time to relax, have a drink at the bar, and make yourself comfortable.

Typically, a host will give a short welcome speech to let you know what to expect. Once the dating part of the evening starts, those with badge number one will start at table number one, those with badge number two at table number two and so on. After a few minutes, the host will ring a bell or blow a whistle, the girls will stay seated and all the guys will move round one table. This continues (with a half time break) until you have met everyone there.

You will probably like a number of people you meet and date at a speed dating evening - the difficulty is choosing who you would really like to see again.

After the Speed Dating event

After the event, simply sign on to the web site and choose the people you would like to see again.

After you have entered your choices, you will be automatically sent an email and/or a text message whenever someone matches with you, with their details. Via the website, you will also be able to see how many people have entered their choices, how many have ticked you and who has matched with you. Chances are that you will be pleasantly surprised as to how many matches you will get.

Other things to note

About a third of attendees on a typical night come on their own, and most other people who arrive on their own will welcome you chatting to them too.

Generally an event will last just over two hours including a twenty minute half time breather.

It is generally advisable to dress 'Smart Casual', so wear what you are comfortable with - jeans and a smart top are fine - but don't forget that first impressions count! It is not a fashion show, but above all - be yourself!

Chapter 3: What questions should you ask

Voltaire said *Judge a man by his questions rather than his answers.*

Here you will find a list of 250 speed dating questions - quite probably the largest collection of speed dating questions anywhere. These questions will help you find out more about your dates, help you get to know them, to see if you have any common interests, to see if there is any chemistry, and to see if the spark is there - or not.

You couldn't possibly ask all of these questions in one go, so we recommend choosing just five of these questions and memorising them. If it is easier for you, write them down on a piece of card, or even on your hand and refer to the questions during the evening. After you have asked two or three people your favourite five questions you will probably remember them and won't need to refer to your notes.

We have categorised these 250 speed dating questions into the following: - (1) finding out more about your date; (2) finding out about your dates' hobbies and interests; (3) fun questions and (4) some offbeat questions.

The questions that you choose to use will help to keep the conversation flowing. Just slip your questions into the conversation at an appropriate time during the evening. Remember that speed dating is not a job interview – do listen to the answers you are given and don't keep firing off questions. Instead, the trick is to blend your chosen questions naturally into your chat.

Each speed date could be the beginning of a serious relationship and the best way to find out if the person you are talking to has long term potential for you is to ask them questions that will reveal something about their character and their personality.

If you don't ask questions, you will not find out about the person you are talking to and you will thus never find out if he or she is the one.

So, choose just five questions that are closest to your heart and whose answers are important to you. Remember to blend your questions into your short speed dates, rather than fire the questions off one after another.

Right, let's get onto the speed dating questions.

Chapter 4: Questions to help you find out about your date

- What do you do for fun?

- Where are you from originally?

- What makes you happy?

- Do you have any brothers/sisters?

- How close is your family?

- Do you feel your childhood was happier than most other people's?

- How do you feel about your relationship with your mother?

- If you could change anything about the way you were raised, what would it be?

- What is the largest city you have ever visited?

- How would your best friend describe you?

- What is your dream job?

- What has been your favourite job in the past?

- What are you most passionate about?

- What do you consider your best attribute?

- If you have friends coming for supper what would you cook?

- What's your favourite wine?

- Who has been the biggest inspiration in your life?

- What are the most important things you're looking for in a person?

- Which season of the year do you like most?

- What is the most interesting thing about you?

- Are you a morning or night person?

- What makes you sad?

- Are you always, sometimes or never on time?

- How would your work colleagues describe you?

- How would your friends describe you?

- If you weren't here tonight, what would you be doing?

- What is the craziest thing you've ever done?

- Why did you come here tonight?

- What is your type?

- What makes you angry?

- What's your favourite cocktail?

- Do you have any phobias?

- What was your best weekend this year?

- Did you have a nickname at school?

- Do you have any tattoos?

- Where were you born?

Are you
more of a
city or
country
person?

- What star sign are you?

- Are you a spender or a saver?

- Do you have any piercings?

- Have you ever been mentioned in a newspaper?

- Have you ever stayed up all night talking to someone?

- Do you prefer sweet or salty foods?

- What are you most proud about?

- When did you last cry in front of another person?

- Is religion important to you?

- What is your favourite dish to cook?

- If you could visit anywhere in the world, where would you go?

- What is the one thing that nobody knows about you?

- Are you interested in politics?

- What is one thing you miss about being a child?

- Are you messy, neat or in-between?

- What is your favourite thing to do on a Saturday night?

- What is your favourite thing to do on a Sunday morning?

- What is your most treasured possession?

- How often do you check your email?

- For what in your life do you feel most grateful?

- What do you value most in a friendship?

- What makes you laugh?

- What is your biggest peeve?

- What was the best year of your life?

- Are you good with your money or frivolous?

- Where did you spend your last birthday?

- Where did you spend last New Year's Eve?

- What is your favourite takeaway meal?

- Where did you study?

- What do you normally have for breakfast?

- What was your favourite childhood television program?

- Are you a light or heavy sleeper?

- Have you ever been on TV?

- Do you consider yourself introverted or extroverted

- Are you most like earth, wind, fire or water?

- Are you a night owl or an early bird?

- What birthstone are you?

Choosing questions from this category will give you a good understanding of your date's personality. Their answers would have given you an insight into their character. Now let's move on to what makes them tick.

Chapter 5: Questions to find out about your dates' hobbies and interests

- What did you do last weekend?

- What kind of music do you like?

- What's your favourite food?

- What was the last CD you bought / music track you downloaded?

- What's the favourite country you've ever visited?

- What TV show is unmissable for you?

- Do you enjoy cooking?

- Which do you prefer: a walk in the countryside or sat in front of the TV relaxing?

- What period of history most intrigues you?

- What kind of movies do you like?

- What sports do you enjoy or follow?

- What's your number one hobby?

- Do you like to gamble?

- What is your favourite film?

- Who is your favourite actor/actress?

- Which is your favourite genre of movies - comedy/thriller/action?

- What was the last film you saw?

- What is your favourite TV programme?

- Can you play a musical instrument?

- What types of books do you like to read?

- What was the last book you bought?

- What book are you reading at the moment?

- Do you like to go shopping?

- Do you have a pet?

- How many email addresses do you have?

- Can you change a tyre?

- Do you like to dance?

- What is your favourite restaurant?

- Beach break or winter break?

- Do you like outdoorsy activities?

- Do you prefer exploring or lazing on the beach?

- Who is you favourite sporting hero?

- What is your favourite book?

- Have you ever done a bungee jump?

- As a child, what was your favourite book?

- Are you an outdoors or indoors person?

How do you spend your spare time?

- Do you like going to museums?

- Have you ever been travelling? And if so where to?

- Do you like animals?

- Would you prefer to climb a mountain or trek across a desert?

- Do you believe in astrology?

- DIY or call an expert?

- Do you ever go the gym?

- Do you ski?

- Do you prefer an active or a lazing around holiday?

- What is the best concert you have ever been to?

Choosing questions from this hobbies and interests category will have given you an understanding of what your date likes to do for fun. You will be able to judge if there are any shared interests between the two of you. Now let's move on to some questions to explore a little more about their personality.

Chapter 6: Some real fun speed dating questions

- Would you like to be famous?

- What would you take with you to a desert island?

- If you could be someone else for a day, who would you be?

- If you could invite anyone, dead or alive, to dinner, who would it be?

- If I gave you £50,000 right now for you to have an adventure, where would you go?

- What would be your ideal holiday destination?

- What's the most reckless thing you've ever done?

- Do you have a bucket list?

- If you were to perform in the circus, what would you do?

- Which celebrity would you most like to have sex with?

- Do you suffer from road rage?

- If you could do any job in the world, what would you do?

- On a scale of 1-10, how attractive would you say you are?

- Do you sing in the shower?

- When it comes to decorating, what's your style?

- If you could go on an adventure anywhere in the world, where would you go?

- What colour best describes your personality?

- What is the funniest thing that you have seen in the past month?

- If you had to be someone else for a day, who would it be?

- If a film was made about your life, who would you like to play you?

- What would the title of your autobiography be?

- Who was your hero, as a child?

- Who is your hero nowadays?

- Which is the one job in the world that you would love to do?

- What song best sums you up?

- What, if anything, is too serious to be joked about?

- Your home catches fire. After saving your loved ones and pets, you have time to save just one item. What would it be?

- If you could choose the sex of your child, would you do it?

- Do you believe in love at first sight?

- Would you rather be rich or have true love?

- If you were an animal in the wild, what would you be?

- What is your favourite month of the year and why?

- If you could travel back in time, what would you change?

- If you were to advertise yourself on a billboard, what would your slogan be?

- If you were granted three wishes what would they be?

Who was the first crush you ever had?

- What car would you have if money was no object?

- What is your favourite word?

- If you were stranded on a desert island, what three items would you most want?

- If you won the lottery, what would you do?

- Have you ever Googled yourself?

- What's the most crazy, reckless thing you've ever done?

- If you had to move to a foreign city for one year, where would it be?

- Would you run with the bulls at Pamplona?

- You're in a karaoke bar - which song do you sing?

- Would you be willing to have horrible nightmares for a year if you would be rewarded with extraordinary wealth?

- If you could live anywhere in the world where would it be?

- If you could commit one crime without being caught, what would it be?

- Will you tell me a secret?

- What was the first thing you notice about the opposite sex?

- What is the worst chat up line you know?

- In one word, how would your friends describe you?

- Do you have any claims to fame?

- Who is your favourite person on the planet?

- Would you rather know your future or change your past?

- What food have you eaten too much of in your life?

- If you could invite three famous people to dinner, who would they be?

- What time in history would you have liked to be born in and why?

- What's the one thing you've wanted to do, but never have?

- If you were to star in a movie, who would you like as your co-star?

- What is the most adventurous thing you have ever done?

- What would be the title of your biography?

- Into which personality's shoes would you like to step for a day?

- Who is you favourite actor/actress/celebrity?

- If you could have any type of pet, what would it be?

- Do you believe in miracles?

- What is your best chat up line?

- What would be your perfect holiday?

- If you ruled the world, what would you change?

- Have you ever met a celebrity?

- Would you rather be healthy or wealthy?

- What is the cheesiest chat up line you have heard?

- What's your best joke?

- How old were you when you had your first kiss?

- What would constitute a perfect day for you?

- What is the one thing about yourself that you would like me to know?

- If your friends compared you to an animal, which animal would it be?

- If you could wake up tomorrow having gained one quality or ability, what would it be?

- Do you have a party trick?

- Are you ticklish?

- You have got six months to live, what will you do first?

- If you were given £1,000 tomorrow, what would you spend it on?

- In your eyes, what is the worst of the seven deadly sins?

- Which of the seven dwarfs are you most like?

Choosing questions from this category will have given you an understanding of what your date likes to do for fun. From the answers given, you will no doubt be able to see if there is any compatibility between the two of you. Now let's move on to some oddball questions to see what they are really all about.

Chapter 7: Great offbeat questions to help break the ice

- If you were invisible, what would you do?

- If a movie was made about your life, who would you want to play you?

- Do you snore?

- If you were in the Hunger Games, would you make it out alive?

- What is your favourite type of cheese?

- When you were a child, did you like to climb trees?

- Who is your favourite Star Wars character?

- If you were on death row, what would your last meal be?

- Have you ever locked your keys in your car?

- Do you believe in UFOs?

- Do you agree with the death penalty?

- Do you believe in ghosts?

- If you found out that you only had 6 months to live, how would you spend those 6 months?

- What is your biggest fear?

- What is your first thought when you wake up?

- Do you obey the speed limit?

- Should a tree be pruned, or left to nature?

- Before making a phone call, do you ever rehearse what you're going to say?

- Which would you prefer, dancing in a hot club or privately under the stars?

- If you had to be a piece of fruit, what would you be?

- How would you like to be remembered?

- Are you a hoarder, or do you throw things away?

- Do you believe in life after death?

- Do you think about past lovers?

- Do you have a recurring dream?

- What's the weirdest dream you have ever had?

- Have you ever been to jail?

- Have you ever had a near death experience?

- Chunky or smooth - as in peanut butter?

- What's the strangest question someone else has asked you tonight?

- If you were a bird, what type of bird would you be?

- What is your stance on cannibalism? For or against?

- If you were an alien and you could abduct anyone on earth, who would you abduct?

- If you could be stuck on a desert island with anyone, who would you pick?

Do you believe in life on other planets?

- Have you ever had a one night stand?

- Is there something that you've dreamt of doing for a long time? Why haven't you done it?

- If a crystal ball could tell you the truth about the future, what would you want to know?

- Have you ever been told that you look like someone famous?

- If you were cremated, where would you like your ashes to be scattered?

- What would you like written on your tombstone?

- If you were a jelly bean, what flavour would you be?

- What secret super power would you most like to have?

There are plenty of very good speed dating questions there - and as before we recommend you choose just five for your evening. Don't take a long list with you - just have a few questions to ease the conversations along and find out more about the people you are talking to, and remember at all times to Have Fun!

The final bonus
question is the
author's favourite: -

What is the most
beautiful place in the
world you have ever
been?

About the author

Connor Champion is a nom de plume for award winning author Carl Christensen - who set up and run Slow Dating, which was for many years the UK's favourite speed dating company. He has hosted and overseen many speed dating evenings and has seen numerous relationships develop as a result of people meeting at Slow Dating events.

Hopefully, this book is going to be useful for you. I do hope you enjoyed reading this book, and if you did, would you kindly take a moment to review the book on Amazon.

Many thanks in advance.